Printed in the United States of America

ISBN-13: 978-0-15-352849-1
ISBN-10: 0-15-352849-4

1 2 3 4 5 6 7 8 9 10 179 11 10 09 08 07 06

Visit *The Learning Site!* www.harcourtschool.com

The Roots of American Music

In the South, people from many different places came together to create a new culture. An important part of that culture was music. Many of the musical styles in the United States began in the South. Different groups of people there created the first truly American music.

Some of the early settlers of the South were from Scotland and Ireland. They lived in the Appalachian Mountains. Their traditional music included songs that told long stories, called ballads. The music for ballads was played on a violin, also called a fiddle. This folk music was very different from the music listened to by most early Americans.

This illustration shows a fiddler playing traditional music.

The banjo began as an African instrument. When slaves came to America, they made banjos to play here.

In other parts of the South, plantation owners brought enslaved Africans to the United States. These Africans brought their own musical traditions to this country.

Slaves had to face terrible hardships. Singing songs helped them deal with their difficult lives. Their music had complicated beats. The instruments they made and played were based on African instruments.

The lives of settlers in the Appalachian Mountains and of slaves on plantations almost never crossed. But as time passed, music from the different groups began to mix. This musical mixture grew into the first music invented in the United States. These new musical styles could only have been created in the South, where very different cultures came together.

The Spirit of the Blues

Enslaved people often sang while they worked. Over time, African American slaves became Christians. Soon many of their songs started to be about stories from the Bible. These songs were called spirituals.

Some spirituals were based on the music of the slave owners. But the slaves added parts of their own. Sometimes they changed the words as they went along. Often one singer called out the words, and other singers answered.

After the Civil War, the subject of spiritual songs began to change. Some African Americans began singing about how hard life was for them in the South. This new music was called the blues.

African American slaves began to sing spirituals based on stories from the Bible.

Blues music reminds some people of a feeling. They say they "feel blue" when they are sad. Blues music is often about sad times in a person's life.

The words in the blues songs were repeated over and over, and the music was never written down. Blues musicians often made up the music as they played. These ideas came from African music.

One of the most important centers for the blues was the Mississippi Delta. This is the triangle-shaped area around the mouth of the Mississippi River. In the Delta, blues guitarists slid a glass bottleneck up and down the strings. This made the notes sound almost like a person crying.

Blues musicians Muddy Waters and Otis Spann

Jazz Music

Most of the time, blues songs were sung and played by just one musician with a guitar. Then in New Orleans, Louisiana, African American musicians mixed dance music with the blues. They started playing in a new way.

The musicians in these bands played horns, such as the trumpet, trombone, and saxophone. They played blues songs without singing any of the words. Each musician would take a turn playing an improvised, or made-up, part called a solo.

This style of music became very popular, and many bands started playing it. They called their new music jazz. No one had ever heard anything quite like it.

Buddy Bolden and other musicians in New Orleans (above) turned blues music into jazz. Often jazz musicians would play in the streets of New Orleans. They still do this today (below).

Louis Armstrong

People visited New Orleans from all over the country. Tourism introduced visitors to the new jazz music that was being played there. Soon people in other parts of the country wanted to hear jazz. The first jazz recording was made by a group of New Orleans musicians called the Original Dixieland Jazz Band. Their record was a huge hit.

One of the most famous musicians to play jazz music was Louis Armstrong. He took the New Orleans music to big cities like Chicago, New York, and Los Angeles. Soon people all over the country were listening to jazz on records and on the radio.

Jazz musicians became stars. Different styles of jazz were developed around the world. But the roots of jazz came from New Orleans and its special mix of people.

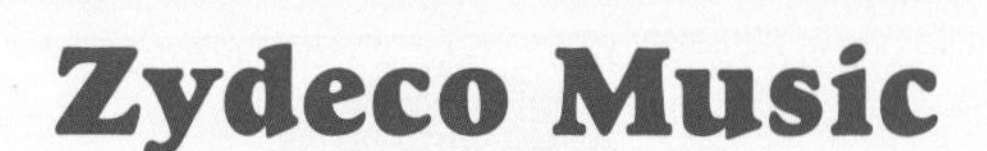

Zydeco Music

Jazz was not the only kind of music that came from Louisiana. France once ruled Louisiana. Under French laws, it was legal for slaves to play music. Because of this, there was more African music played in all parts of Louisiana. This helped create many interesting new styles.

One style was played by Creoles. Creoles were the descendants of slaves who had come from French colonies in the Caribbean. Creole music was made for dancing. Some of the dance steps came from West Africa and the Caribbean islands.

Nathan Williams and his zydeco band

Amanda Shaw: Cajun Fiddler

Cajun music is another style of music from Louisiana. It combines French folk music with European, African, and Native American influences. Cajun music usually features a fiddle player. One of the best young Cajun musicians is fiddler Amanda Shaw from Louisiana.

The mix of cultures in Louisiana made new forms of music possible. But what made a music called zydeco possible was a new instrument—the accordion.

Musicians from Germany brought their accordions to New Orleans. The sound of the accordion, mixed with Creole and blues music, became zydeco music. The words in zydeco songs were sung in French. The music was loud enough to be heard across a crowded dance floor.

For a long time, zydeco music was only played at dances in southwestern Louisiana. Then some zydeco musicians made records. Now zydeco dances are held all across the United States.

Creole sidewalk band in 1921

Country Music

As New Orleans was bursting with music, another kind of music was taking shape in the Appalachian Mountains. This music was being made by people whose ancestors came from Scotland and Ireland. The folk songs these people sang were based on stories about heroes and outlaws.

As time passed, Appalachian music began to mix with blues music. Soon the people in the mountains started singing about different subjects. Like blues singers, they started singing about their own lives and problems. People who heard the music understood the feelings in the songs.

Jimmie Rodgers (left) and the Carter Family (below) took songs that were played in the mountains and recorded them. The songs became very popular.

Ernest Tubb and his band performing at the Grand Ole Opry in 1944

This new form of music was often played with guitars and fiddles. Musicians also used a new instrument called a steel guitar.

For a long time, the music was never recorded or written down. It was mostly played in the mountains, away from the cities of the South. A few musicians began to record these mountain songs. Soon people wanted to hear more of this new music called country music.

In a very short time, country music became very popular. One reason for this was the "Grand Ole Opry." This radio show from Nashville, Tennessee, started playing country music in 1925. Country music stars were heard every week on the show. Nashville became the center for country music.

Bluegrass Music

Once country music became popular, people began to experiment with it and change it. One man, named Bill Monroe, played a kind of country music that was different. It blended folk music with other styles.

Bill Monroe was from Kentucky, the Bluegrass State. He named his country band the Blue Grass Boys.

The Blue Grass Boys played a guitar, a banjo, a fiddle, and a mandolin. These traditional instruments made the band's music sound a lot like the old-time music played in the South before country music. The words that Bill Monroe's band sang were also more traditional. Many songs had no words, only music.

Bill Monroe (right) and his Blue Grass Boys

Bluegrass bands like the Stanley Brothers (above) and Flatt and Scruggs (left) followed in Bill Monroe's footsteps.

Sometimes two singers in the Blue Grass Boys would sing the words at the same time. The singers blended their voices together. This made the new style easy to recognize.

The members of the band were very skilled at playing their instruments. They played very fast. While they played, different musicians would take solos, an idea borrowed from jazz. Soon other groups started playing music in the same style. This style became known as bluegrass, after the name of Bill Monroe's band.

By listening to bluegrass music, you can hear how different styles of music in the South shaped each other. Bluegrass is a mix of country music, Appalachian folk music, and jazz.

Rock and Roll

After World War II, some musicians took the style of the blues and added sounds from country music to it. The words to these new songs were about modern life. This music was called rock and roll.

The instruments used in rock and roll were high-tech for the time. They were almost all electric. Unlike country or jazz bands, which had many different instruments, most rock and roll bands had only guitars and drums.

The first rock and roll musicians were African Americans. They had taken the beats and music of the blues and made them easier to dance to. Musicians like Chuck Berry, Bo Diddley, and Little Richard were some of the first to play rock and roll.

Chuck Berry was one of the first musicians to play the new style called rock and roll.

Sun Records

In the 1950s, Sam Phillips started a record label called Sun Records in Memphis, Tennessee. He wanted to discover new musicians and record their music. The singers he found turned out to be some of the most important musicians in rock and roll history. He recorded Elvis Presley, Johnny Cash, Jerry Lee Lewis, and Carl Perkins. Sun Records was the place where some of the most famous musicians got their start.

Other musicians started playing rock and roll as well. Some of these musicians knew a lot of country music. When they started performing rock and roll, they added parts of country music to their own music.

The most famous early rock and roll singer was Elvis Presley. He had an amazing voice and was a very good dancer. His songs were about things teenagers cared about, like dancing, falling in love, and having fun.

Elvis Presley

Some parents worried that rock and roll would cause young people to behave badly. This just made rock and roll more popular. Other people thought that rock and roll was only a fad and that it would soon disappear. But they were wrong. Rock and roll became the most popular style of music in the world.

Think and Respond

1. Where did the people who settled in the Appalachian Mountains come from?
2. How are blues music and country music different? How are they the same?
3. Where was the first jazz music played?
4. Why do you think so many different kinds of music developed in the South?
5. Why do you think American music is so popular in other parts of the world?

Activity

With two or three of your classmates, imagine that you are in a band together. First, decide on the kind of music you would play. If you like different kinds of music, how could you mix those different kinds of music? Then, write a song, using what you have learned about that style of music.

Photo Credits
Front Cover Yale Joel/Time Life Pictures/Getty Images; 2 The Granger Collection, NY; 3 Corbis; 4 Bettmann/Corbis; 5 Terry Cryer/Corbis; 6 (t) Frank Driggs Collection/Getty Images, (b) Robert Holmes/Corbis; 7 Prints and Photographs Division, Library of Congress; 8 Philip Gould/Corbis; 8-9 Frank Driggs Collection/Getty Images; 9 AP Photo/Bill Haber; 10 (l) Bettmann/Corbis, (r) Eric Schaal/Time Life Pictures/Getty Images; 11 Frank Driggs Collection/Getty Images; 12 AP Photo/The Nashville Banner; 13 (l) Bettmann/Corbis, (r) John Byrne Cooke; 14 Frank Diggs Collection/Getty Images; 15 (t) AP Photo/Mike Brown, (b) Bettmann/Corbis; Back Cover Prints and Photographs Division, Library of Congress.